BARN WEDDINGS

BARN WEDDINGS

MAGGIE LORD

GIBBS SMITH
TO ENRICH AND INSPIRE HUMANKIND

First Edition

17 16 15 14 13   5 4 3 2

Published by

Gibbs Smith

P.O. Box 667

Layton, Utah 84041

1.800.835.4993 orders

www.gibbs-smith.com

Designed by Tracy Johnson

Printed and bound in China

Gibbs Smith books are printed on either recycled, 100%
post-consumer waste, FSC-certified papers or on paper
produced from sustainable PEFC-certified forest/
controlled wood source. Learn more at www.pefc.org.

Library of Congress Cataloging-in-Publication Data

Lord, Maggie.
  Barn weddings / Maggie Lord. — First Edition.
    pages cm
  ISBN 978-1-4236-3165-1
1. Weddings—Planning. I. Title.
  HQ745.L6697 2013
  395.2'2—dc23
                    2013002963

To my earliest and strongest supporters, my brothers, Eddie and Charlie Panian

- -

CONTENTS

ACKNOWLEDGMENTS

- -

No matter the location, size, budget or style, all weddings are dependent on the support of family, friends and loved ones. This book is inspired by all the couples who call upon their families and friends to help make their wedding experience a meaningful journey. No wedding has ever come off successfully without a little elbow grease and determination, much of which is done by the support team around the bride and groom. This book, much like a wedding, is the culmination of both hard work and passion and is made possible by the amazing support team I am surrounded with both personally and professionally.

To Kate McKenna and Maggie Carson Romano for being wonderful style gurus who provide endless amounts of inspiration in a wide variety of forms. To my East Coast freelancers in The 504 who are always ready to help.

Once again, to the team at Gibbs Smith Books, especially my editor, Hollie Keith, who makes the process of creating a book an enjoyable and exciting one.

Thank you to all the wedding vendors and wedding professionals who added their knowledge, artistic abilities and skills to this book. I cannot thank you enough.

To my close friends and family, for all the support they provide.

To my husband, Jon, and our son, Jack, who make my life complete.

And lastly, to my family, who without you, none of this would be possible or worthwhile.

INTRODUCTION

A BARN IS A MAGICAL PLACE FOR A WEDDING. Steeped in history and evoking the simplicity of a place that time has forgotten, the classic American barn has been a subject irresistible to artists, poets, and city folk alike for its stoic visage and endearing presence. Hosting a rustic barn wedding not only allows the betrothed couple the space to gather amongst their nearest and dearest together under one roof, but the pure, utilitarian framework is the basis for a fully customizable wedding aesthetic. Whether a simple celebration of the good life in the countryside or an elegant, sophisticated affair, a barn is the perfect backdrop for a singularly gorgeous wedding day.

Underscored by the history and romance of life on the farm, the barn is an essential part of the American landscape. Straightforward in its construction yet sturdy enough to last for generations, the barn has always been a shelter and gathering place. Set on majestic and peaceful countryside away from the hectic bustle of the city, the barn can't help but suggest a feeling of sanctuary and shelter to all who enter into its warm embrace. The rich history of the structure extends back to European and North American farming families who lived in homes that were attached or integrated into barns. Vermont, in particular, is famous for its farmhouses that connect to the adjacent barns, enabling farm families to care for their livestock during the brutal winter months without ever leaving the protection of the indoors.

Despite the storybook image of the small red barn with white trim perched atop a rolling hill, barn design and architecture varies depending on the traditions of the people the barns served, the conditions to which they had to adapt, and the specific functions for which they were used. The round barns of New England nod to the region's Shaker past, while the large dairy barns of the Midwest maintain the age-old tradition of the red-colored barn. The color stems from the traditional orange-red stain left by linseed oil, often mixed with rust, that farmers once used to treat and seal the wood of a new barn.

Barns were, for many communities, the only venue outside the local church that could house all the townspeople for special events and celebrations.

Dances, lectures, and meetings were all centered around the barn. For a modern couple, a barn wedding harkens back to the old-fashioned tradition of a barn raising. In order to build such an important structure, neighbors and community members rallied together to help build the barn and, in so doing, embodied the maxim that "many hands make light work." For a couple vowing to build a strong and loving marriage, how better to start off married life than with the support of your friends and family to help you rise to the challenge.

Inherent in the choice to have a barn wedding offers a great deal of flexibility and ample room for imagination. Your ceremony and reception can use the barn as a backdrop for a lovely day in the fresh

country air. It can serve as the perfect canvas for an indoor reception, dappled by twinkling lights hung from the rafters and the glow of candles from tables full of loved ones. A barn works equally well as a backup for inclement weather or as the centerpiece of a wedding's design. Part indoor, part outdoor, but all beautiful, historic and romantic, barn weddings are as practical as they are ripe with opportunity for chic charm and creativity.

After writing *Rustic Wedding Chic* I was inspired to explore another style of rustic weddings and showcase the best of what barn weddings have to offer. I hope you find this book as inspiring and magical as it was for me to write.

STYLES

BARNS HAVE A PERSONALITY AND STYLE all their own due to their natural beauty, country charisma, and effortless charm. The right barn can provide the backdrop for a wedding that is sure to stand out from the crowd and be remembered for years to come. From majestic barns in the Northeast to Midwestern diary barns to the quaint backyard barns in the Deep South, each barn is 100 percent unique.

One thing I have heard over the years is that you can't make a barn work for you; you have to make yourself work for the barn. Of course, depending on where you live, the types of barns available to you vary. Since barns are designed for a specific purpose and in a style specific of the region where they are located, sometimes their setup is not ideal for a wedding.

Keeping these limitations in mind, it's important to align yourself with the barn in its natural state in order to see if it might work for you. For example, there are equestrian-style barns that allow for a more refined, English-style wedding. On the other hand, there are more western-style barns that might even come complete with a horse or two. Some barns are just not going to be able to accommodate a large wedding reception with a full dinner and dancing, so it's important to have a vision for your barn wedding style before you try to find a barn that's right for you.

Weddings are inherently elegant no matter the setting, but the way in which you achieve elegance in your barn wedding is up to you. The rustic nature of a barn gives you a chance to curate your wedding from the ground up. By tuning in to some key style elements you want to include, while also paying close attention to factors like the geographical region, barn style, and venue amenities, you will see your personal barn wedding style start to take shape.

BARN WEDDING STYLES

KEEPING IT SIMPLE

If you are going for a simple style for your wedding, the first thing you need to decide is what does simple mean to you? Is it the décor that you want to keep simple? Or maybe you're looking for a simple dinner menu? Or does simple mean you'd like to have a relaxed, stress-free wedding day? In any case, "simple" doesn't mean your choices have to be plain or limited in any way. Sometimes keeping things simple just leaves room for that understated beauty brides so often hope to achieve.

BUDGET FRIENDLY

If you are working with a budget—and let's face it, who isn't? A barn wedding might be perfect for you. A barn offers so much natural beauty that details like large floral arrangements and major décor pieces can be left off the expense list, or at least pared down and simplified in order to allow the natural beauty of the space to shine through.

ECO-FRIENDLY

If you are even considering a barn wedding, chances are you have some eco-friendly ideas in mind. Incorporating eco-friendly aspects into your wedding décor really pays homage to the barn's rustic nature and history and you'll find that it's easy and inexpensive to create décor to match the beauty of the barn.

LEFT: *A brown barn gives a touch of scenery and acts as the backdrop for this outdoor wedding reception.*

FACING: *As evening falls on this barn wedding, a simple but beautiful wedding table is left unattended.*

PAGE 14: *A long and narrow barn is the setting for a wedding cocktail hour. Strands of lights are hung above to add an element of elegance.*

The easiest way to make your wedding day eco-friendly is to take on some simple re-purposing projects. Vintage bottles, cans, and pitchers can be easily transformed into beautiful vases, while old windowpanes, doors and even dressers can become lovely display pieces for menus or seating cards.

Another way to be eco-friendly is by buying locally grown food or hiring local vendors for your wedding day feast. By going local, you're not only supporting small businesses, but you're also introducing your wedding guests to the best of what your wedding location has to offer. Everything from locally grown corn to cranberries can be served and you can add treats like pies from a local farm stand to sweeten the evening. If you're really taken with a local product and have the budget, send guests home with favors like local honey or jam.

The large carbon footprint left by a wedding is one reason why couples are choosing to work with nature rather than against it. So keep your barn wedding eco-friendly by letting your creativity shine with a few repurposing projects or exploring the local community for treats! No matter what you do, you'll be saving money and saving the planet!

TOP: *Small jars of jam are dressed up with burlap and tags that read: "spread the love." They are given to guests as favors.*

CENTER: *A repurposed window is cleverly turned into a wedding menu and displayed for guests to see as they enter the reception venue.*

LEFT: *A large floral arrangement is surrounded by small wedding details such as buttons, multicolored thread and vintage linens.*

LAVISH SOPHISTICATION

There is nothing wrong with fulfilling your wedding day fantasy and having a lavish and sophisticated affair. If crystal chandeliers, white tablecloths, and endless amounts of romantic candlelight are what you envision, then go ahead and start planning because even a barn can be dressed up to meet every wedding day expectation you might have.

So just how do you "dress up" a barn? It's one of the questions brides most frequently ask me. My simple answer is to first add lighting. Lighting is necessary, but when done in the right way, it can add drama to any setting. Whether you decide to hang strings of lights, scatter lanterns around, or invest in a lighting company to come and spotlight the space, it's all up to you. With the right light, you really are able to make the space feel as intimate as you like.

Secondly, you need to bring in the color white. Adding the color white helps to break up the dark, wooden framework of a barn, while adding a bright, weightlessness to the space. Try hanging long white drapes at the barn entrance or throughout the space. White tablecloths will bring a focal point to the large, open space and make the setting feel more intimate.

I always remind brides that lavish does not necessarily mean expensive and that you can still achieve a lavish style without a big price tag. Depending on the barn you choose, it might be up to you to find creative ways to convert it into the elegant venue you desire. The right lighting and some white accents can go a long way in transforming any barn into a beautiful space.

ABOVE LEFT: Letting elements in nature act as wedding displays is one of the best parts of having a rustic-style wedding. These tree stumps allow an array of lanterns to be showcased.

ABOVE RIGHT: Outdoor lighting is a must for any kind of country or rustic wedding. A twist on the traditional white lights, these lantern-style lights are functional and rustic.

TYPES OF BARN VENUES & THE GEOGRAPHIC REGION

In choosing the right barn for your wedding, you must also consider whether you're looking for a private barn or a more commercial wedding venue. There is no right or wrong in this situation and the choice is yours to make, but each comes with its own set of considerations.

If you are lucky enough to either have your own barn or know someone who is willing to let you use a barn, then you have already eliminated the first headache of trying to find a venue. When planning a barn wedding on private property, you might have complete décor freedom, but you also have some additional considerations that you would not have if you were holding your wedding at an established barn wedding venue. It really comes down to the logistics when planning a wedding at a private residence. First of all, will the space be able to accommodate all your guests? Next, does the layout of the barn work for the type of wedding you would like to have? Once these major questions are answered, you can tackle specifics like providing lighting, heating or cooling, bathrooms, and food service.

Some private barns will need a lot more logistical work than others. If your wedding will be taking place on a working farm, I suggest you visit the farm several times and, if possible, visit in the same season that your wedding will take place. This way, you can be aware of season-specific things such as animals and, without going into detail, all that goes along with that. Of course, every barn is different, so it will be up to you to assess what the space needs and get to work making it happen.

If you are like most of us and don't have a private barn available to you, many farms, museums, and historical institutions already have barn-like venues available for rent. Some of them are more classic barns, while others have been repurposed with modern facilities. If you have chosen to say "I do" and celebrate at an established barn wedding venue, you won't have the same questions as someone who is essentially starting from scratch. There are still some things to take into consideration. Although you'll eliminate many of the worries that come with planning and hosting a wedding privately by choosing an established venue, you will have to adhere to the rules of the venue. This might limit your possibilities in terms of things like décor and the flow of the day, so make sure you communicate clearly with the venue about what you want and that you understand exactly what the venue can offer.

For more venue ideas, check out RusticWedding Guide.com.

ABOVE: *A more contemporary barn structure with dark wood and green trim shelters this bride and groom.*

RIGHT: *Barns are not only the perfect place for large wedding receptions, but they can also be the perfect spot for the actual wedding ceremony. With dramatic lighting and drapery, this seemingly unpolished space is transformed into a sophisticated venue.*

INSPIRATION

- -

EVERY WEDDING STARTS WITH AN INSPIRATION, however big or small. Your inspiration could be something as simple as a piece of fabric, a color scheme, or an image from a magazine. Or maybe it's still just an image in your mind, a fantasy you've had since childhood. Whatever it may be, it's a place to start. All weddings begin with a simple vision that grows into a beautiful event. For those seeking inspiration, wedding inspiration shoots offer highly styled examples of different wedding themes and décor. Wedding inspiration shoots are the dreamy building blocks that often help couples define a wedding style and find creative ways to start planning and personalizing their own special day. The wedding inspiration shoots featured in this section are built around a specific theme and offer a more focused look at the particular details of barn wedding style.

STARS & STRIPES

CLASSIC AMERICANA STYLE TAKES CENTER STAGE
IN THIS PICNIC SHOOT THAT FEATURES STARS AND STRIPES
AND IS PAIRED WITH SUBTLE TOUCHES OF RED, WHITE
AND BLUE ACCENTS. COMPLETE WITH RETRO SODA BOTTLES
AND AMUSING LAWN GAMES, THIS COUNTRY FARM SHOOT
SHOWS OFF AN ALL-AMERICAN NOSTALGIA FEELING.

TOGETHER WITH THEIR FAMILIES
ANNA *and* TYLER
MORGAN WALKINS
INVITE YOU TO CELEBRATE THEIR MARRIAGE
JULY 13, 2012
AT HALF PAST SIX O'CLOCK IN THE EVENING
Riverside Yacht Club

RSVP
BY JUNE 18, 2012

WE'LL BE THERE TO TOAST TO Y'ALL! WE CAN'T
WAIT FOR THIS _____ UP US TO KICK UP OUR
HEELS TO OUR FAVORITE DANCING SONG.

_____ SADLY, WE'LL MISS Y'ALL.

PLEASE DELIVER TO
ANNA *and* TYLER
MORGAN WALKINS
3478 VANDERBILT DR
NASHVILLE, TN 37864

TRAVEL *delights*

FACING, TOP: *This wedding invitation suite is upbeat with its red, white and blue color theme and with the addition of patterns and shapes.*

FACING, BOTTOM: *Simple everyday items like berries can make for fun and colorful wedding décor items.*

ABOVE: *A vintage item such as a book brings some personality to wedding pictures and creates a less formal look.*

PAGE 22: *Sun fills this barn as an elegant white and green table is set and ready to welcome guests.*

PAGE 24: *Vintage-style items line the shores of this lake and create a one-of-a-kind wedding.*

ABOVE: *An updated twist on a classic white wedding cake stands proudly on a vintage-style suitcase.*

ABOVE RIGHT: *Traditional-style bridal parties can look great when they take on individual styles.*

FACING: *Using items like suitcases can make for a unique motif that can be shown in a wide variety of decorations.*

ABOVE: *A dinner menu is attached to the table setting with a small flag for fun.*

ABOVE RIGHT: *Wedding ring pillows come in all shapes and sizes, but this one with country-style flowers and a simple pattern is both subtle and appropriate.*

ABOVE: *Simple paper can be dressed up with just the right color or pattern.*

ABOVE RIGHT: *White flowers are wrapped with twine to create a perfect country wedding bouquet.*

FACING, TOP LEFT: *This all-American nautical theme brings an upbeat and spirited look to the day.*

FACING, TOP RIGHT: *A wooden long table helps to bring out a classic country feeling.*

FACING, BOTTOM: *Simple table runners paired with monochrome flowers are beautiful yet simple.*

ABOVE: *An unassuming stool acts as the perfect drink display at a country-style wedding.*

ABOVE RIGHT: *Standing among the trees, this bride and groom evoke the perfect country-style wedding.*

ABOVE: *Common and unusual glass soda bottles can be turned into a beautiful flower display.*

FACING: *One the biggest trends in rustic-style barn weddings is the addition of lawn games to the wedding reception.*

FACING: *A red, white and blue theme is carried out in all aspects, even incorporating the drinks.*

ABOVE: *Cream, white and blue dresses look beautiful when paired together.*

FACING, TOP: *Nothing is more important than a couple enjoying their wedding day.*

FACING, BOTTOM LEFT: *Kraft paper place cards are tied to chairs to create a less formal feeling.*

FACING, BOTTOM RIGHT: *Stacked suitcases create the perfect unique wedding display and bring an antique look to the wedding style.*

LEFT: *Classic chalkboards make for fun photo props even for the bride and groom.*

SOURCES

photography: Kristyn Hogan / venue: Old Hickory Lake / event design, styling and paper goods: Amber Housley / floral designs: Brocade Designs / makeup: Amy Lynn Larwig / hair styling: Ashlea Hunter / cake: Crumb de la Crumb / vintage pieces: Jenni Bowlin / lace bolero jacket: Monique Lhuillier / bridesmaid dresses: Monique Lhuiller / menswear: Billy Reid / ring pillow: Hey Babe Studio

VINTAGE COUNTRY AFFAIR

THE BOLD CLASSIC RED BARN SETS THE PERFECT BACKDROP
FOR A SINGLE FARM TABLE SET FOR A VINTAGE COUNTRY
CELEBRATION. WITH THE HELP OF REPURPOSED ITEMS
INCLUDING SUITCASES WHICH MAKE A PERFECT DISPLAY
PIECE AND AN END TABLE SET UP AS A CAKE STAND,
THIS INSPIRATION SHOOT BRINGS TO LIFE A FLEA MARKET
SHOPPERS DREAM. HELPING TO COMPLETE THE VINTAGE
CHIC LOOK ARE STANDOUT PIECES SUCH AS MISMATCHED
CHAIRS, SIMPLE FLORAL SWAGS AND A FEW PIECES OF LACE.

RIGHT: *A vintage-style side table is repurposed as a wedding cake display.*

FACING, TOP: *A classic red barn is the backdrop of this mismatched vintage-style wedding reception.*

FACING, BOTTOM LEFT: *I've found that white flowers always work best when working with a red-colored barn, since they are the perfect complement to the vibrant color.*

FACING, BOTTOM RIGHT: *Four rustic wedding bouquets stand ready to make their appearance.*

PAGE 41: *The mix of white chairs and green chairs with the natural wood table really pop against the red barn backdrop.*

ABOVE: *One tall and simple flower arrangement acts as the main centerpiece for the entire table.*

ABOVE RIGHT: *A simple wood sign acts as a directional indicator for guests.*

FACING: *With a rustic-style background, this bride and groom make for the perfect rustic chic wedding couple.*

- -

PAGE 44, TOP: *A swag of greenery stands out from the rustic background.*

PAGE 44, BOTTOM: *Unique backdrops like this log cabin-style building can be the perfect setting for a wedding ceremony.*

PAGE 45: *Add the mismatched style to your wedding by mixing and matching chairs at your head table. This might be as easy as using chairs from your own home and then calling on your friends and family to fill in with the rest.*

SOURCES

photography: Tahni Candelaria-Holm of Joyeuse
Photography / venue: Rounton Farm / co-stylist
and event coordinator: Cody Grannis, Amore
Events by Cody / hair and makeup: Amanda
Scott / vintage furniture: Shabby Love / antique
items: Gypsy Willow, LionShare Antiques,
Salvage Wrights, Bushwick Hardware / cake
design: Greenock Bakery / catering: Beggars
Banquet / floral design: Colonial Florist / lighting:
Gibson Rental

SOUTHWESTERN STYLE SOIREE

- -

Nothing makes a southwestern style celebration
come to life more than pops of color and
festive decorations. This fiesta style wedding
inspiration blends together a traditional
barn wedding with a ranch style location.
By weaving energetic color choices throughout the
decorations, flowers, bridesmaid dresses and
centerpieces, this wedding comes to life.

FACING, TOP: *A festive wedding centerpiece creates a Mexican-style wedding reception look.*

FACING, BOTTOM: *Striped table linens with pops of color may not seem like the perfect barn wedding décor, yet they bring out a more playful side to a reception.*

ABOVE: *The vibrant color motif is shown in the wedding ceremony decorations, the wedding bouquets and the bridesmaids' dresses.*

PAGE 49: *An impromptu tent is created with ribbons to capture a camp-style wedding image.*

FACING: Having guests wave ribbons is an original way to add a dramatic close to a wedding ceremony.

ABOVE: Complete with a country-style quilt and a barefoot bride, this image captures a relaxed moment.

FACING, TOP: *When you get married in a barn location, you might just have a horse or two as a guest.*

FACING, BOTTOM: *Adding some of the "natural" surroundings into your wedding pictures makes for unforgettable photos.*

LEFT: *A traditional Mexican-style hat is added as a fun photo prop.*

SOURCES

photography: Melissa McCrotty Photography / venue: Barn at Twin Oaks Ranch / hair: La House of Beaute / makeup: MaRya Hunnicutt from Vspa / dresses and tuxedos: Formal Affairs / cake and cookies: Lauren with The Cake Place

GRACEFUL DRAMA

Long flowing white drapes add ultimate drama
and elegance to this rustic barn wedding
inspiration shoot. Featuring only a few standout
decorations like a banner of white flags
and a chandelier wrapped with greenery,
this inspiration shoot demonstrates how
a few key décor pieces can really go a long way.
The impeccable use of white allows for
muted barn wood to be dressed up and transitions
the space into a suitable wedding venue.

FACING: *Barns are sometimes just one large space, so creating smaller areas with simple decorations can help to make the space feel more intimate.*

LEFT: *Short white wedding dresses can be the perfect choice for a barn wedding since many barn locations are true to their rustic roots.*

PAGE 57: *Long white drapes frame the entrance to the barn and set the stage for an elegant wedding at a rustic venue.*

above: A celebratory farewell send-off for the bride and groom as they leave their barn wedding hand in hand.

above right: White flag banners construct a pleasant mood to an otherwise large and open barn.

ABOVE: *White table linens, white chairs and white banner flags create a simple color theme and warm up the muted barn interior.*

ABOVE RIGHT: *A lace-and-fringe shawl keeps this bride warm while her sensibly-selected sandals keep her feet from hurting.*

ABOVE: *Against the natural barn wood stands a blushing bride with a stunning bouquet and a flower hair accessory.*

FACING: *A colorful wedding cake becomes the main focal point when placed against a muted barn and utilitarian-style table.*

SOURCES

photography: Melissa McCrotty Photography / venue: Barn at Twin Oaks Ranch / hair: La House of Beaute / makeup: MaRya Hunnicutt from Vspa / dresses and tuxedos: Formal Affairs / cake and cookies: Lauren with The Cake Place

SOMETHING BLUE

A beautiful light blue color is the major décor element in this romantic barn wedding inspiration. Structuring the entire event around one color, from the invitations to the aisle runner, allows for the theme to take center stage. By adding a strong and vibrant color theme, this inspiration shoot demonstrates how a barn can be taken from just a rustic setting to a stunning wedding location. This inspiration shoot also features a classic country seating option, hay bales, made to feel more elegant with beautiful fabric draped over the tops.

MENU

STARTER: Fried Green Tomato with Lump Crab

DINNER: Roasted Rosemary Chicken with Garlic Mashed Potato and Sauteed Spinach

DESSERT: Wedding Cake and Crumbteenies

WITH MUCH HAPPINESS YOU ARE INVITED TO THE WEDDING OF

Elisa and Grant

05.07.11

HALF PAST SIX IN THE EVENING · SOUTHALL EDEN
3270 SOUTHALL ROAD · FRANKLIN · TENNESSEE

NAME

Yes
No

YOUR SONG REQUEST:

ABOVE: *Blush-toned wedding flowers look perfect in a small blue canning jar.*

ABOVE RIGHT: *Mason jars can be used in hundreds of different ways but one of the favorites among brides is converting them into a country-style chandelier.*

FACING: *Classic country scenery surrounds the dining area of this outdoor wedding reception.*

PAGE 65: *This barn wedding ceremony converts a classic barn into a magical wedding venue.*

PAGE 66: *The new Mrs. and Mr. are surrounded by beautiful rustic wedding details such as hanging mason jar lights, bistro string lights and appropriately decorated chairs.*

PAGE 67, TOP LEFT: *Repurposed items like apple crates painted white along with a few other choice objects form an effortless-looking display area that is fun and functional.*

PAGE 67, TOP RIGHT: *A simple chalkboard is transformed into a country wedding menu display and is in keeping with the cream-and-turquoise color palette.*

PAGE 67, BOTTOM: *An elegant wedding invitation in a turquoise-and-brown color palette invite guests to a country-chic wedding.*

ABOVE: *Adding a sign to your chair is the perfect place to proudly display your new title of "Mrs."*

ABOVE LEFT: *Welcome your guests to your wedding day with hand-painted signs in your wedding day colors. If this do-it-yourself project is more than you want to take on, enlist the help of crafty family members, bridesmaids and friends.*

FACING: *Hay bales are the perfect seating solution to open spaces like barn venues. Adding a covering such as a quilt or a piece of fabric will make the perch more comfortable for your guests.*

THIS PAGE: *Small touches of color are added to a variety of aspects in this wedding, including a reservation sign, ribbon-wrapped flowers on barn poles, the groom's boutonnière and even in the bride's lip color.*

FACING: *A monogram backdrop is constructed to act as the backdrop for the barn wedding ceremony.*

ABOVE: *A classic-looking hanging chandelier along with other wedding details such as a lemonade station and mason jar lights help to shape an elegant wedding look while playing up the country setting.*

FACING: *A brief moment of relaxation for a bride and groom can make for a less formal wedding portrait.*

FACING: *A beautiful bride with a pastel floral bouquet stands elegantly in front of a red barn with white drapes.*

LEFT: *A flower girl with a balloon is ready to make her way into a classic-style barn for a wedding reception.*

SOURCES

photography: Brooke Boling / venue: Southall Eden / floral design: The Enchanted Florist / event design and coordination: Southall Eden / cake and desserts: Crumb de la Crumb / stationery: Southall Eden / dress: Reem Acra / flower girl dress: Waters and Waters from B. Hughes Bridal / hair and makeup: Neil Robison

DÉCOR

DECORATING FOR A BARN WEDDING
is not unlike decorating for any other type of wedding. Couples want the décor to reflect their individual personality, while also playing to the style and beauty of the location. The raw and rustic beauty of a barn offers couples a chance to personalize their wedding day from the ground up. Barns can be made to look as simple or as elegant as you like; all it takes are a few design elements to start the transformation. It's a challenge to strike the perfect balance between the natural beauty of the barn and the stylistic enhancements you need to make in order to create the feeling you want for your wedding day. In this section, we've broken down some of the major design elements and put together some beautiful examples to inspire you as you start to picture your ideal décor.

FLOWERS

One of the most visible style elements at any wedding is the flowers. From flowers on the table to the bouquets that the wedding party and the bride carry, flowers make a statement. When choosing flowers, one of the benefits of having a barn wedding is the fact that you have great height to work with. Since most barns have a beautiful framework of posts and beams, there is an opportunity to incorporate those architectural features into your floral design. Hanging flowers from the barn's posts raises the focal point to eye level. Get creative and try hanging tin vases or wrapping garlands around the posts. Make your tablescape more dynamic by using vases with a variety of heights, a stylistic choice that always works well in a barn.

THIS PAGE, CLOCKWISE FROM TOP LEFT:
Floral arrangements can be made to look country chic when placed in a white pitcher-style vase and with the addition of small accents like twine.

Using all of the structural elements available in the barn, this wedding couple hung floral arrangements on the post of the barn.

Small vases are lined up in a row down a long wedding table.

A wreath is hanging at the entrance of a barn wedding and seems to come to life with the beauty of the white lights behind it.

PAGE 78: *Vintage-style table linens are a wonderful alternative to run-of-the-mill rental linens. Finding vintage tablecloths may be as easy as looking at flea markets, antiques stores, second-hand stores and even your own attic.*

TABLES

Gone are the days when that round table for eight to ten guests is the only table available for your reception. Today's couples are looking to change things up with different table shapes and configurations to make their reception distinct. Long, rectangular tables have really come into fashion for barn weddings because they create a family-style atmosphere and are a great nod to the classic farm table. Long tables are also great for barn spaces because they work well for the layout and are very versatile in terms of the number of guests they can accommodate.

If you prefer round tables, you might consider arranging them so that they are not just randomly spaced. Try grouping them close together in clusters of three or four with a space in between each cluster. By grouping the round tables together in a cluster, you encourage your guests to mingle and socialize with other guests at the tables close to them. Some other table shapes you may want to consider are smaller square tables that fit four and perhaps even a sweetheart table for two for the newly married couple.

SEATING

Seating is necessary at any wedding venue regardless of location and style. One thing you have going for you when planning a barn wedding is that you don't have to go so traditional with your seating choice. Wooden chairs, long benches, pews, or even hay bales can all add to the charm of your barn wedding décor.

ABOVE LEFT: *Small goodie bags for guests look great with the couple's names and the phrase "sweet treats" printed on them.*

ABOVE RIGHT: *Long tables with white linens and table runners create a clean-looking style for this barn wedding reception.*

PLACE SETTINGS

Whether you are having an informal BBQ buffet-style meal or a fancy seven-course feast, it is the small details that can bring flair to your tablescape. The place settings at your reception are a great way to add some small touches that can make a major impact. Tie your silverware with a small ribbon and bow for a country-chic feeling or use napkins in a variety of colors or patterns for that vintage "mismatched" look.

ABOVE LEFT: *A kraft paper wedding menu features a fun theme: Eat, Drink, Be Married!*

ABOVE: *Silverware is tied with a pretty ribbon and placed next to each place setting.*

FACING, LEFT: *Classic rustic directional signs are stationed to greet guests as they arrive and provide much needed information.*

FACING, TOP RIGHT: *A wooden wedding sign can be a great do-it-yourself project and a fun way to establish the wedding venue as your own.*

FACING, BOTTOM RIGHT: *If your ceremony and reception are in two different areas of a wedding venue, you might want to consider pointing your guests in the right direction with a wooden directional sign.*

WOOD SIGNS

Since barns and farms usually come together as a package deal, your wedding may be taking place in a large area and the actual ceremony and reception locations might not be self-explanatory. Pointing your guests in the right direction is not only a nice gesture, but more importantly it ensures that your wedding day will start on time. If some directional signs are a necessity, make them fun! Making wooden signs can be a great DIY project because it allows you to make something that reflects your taste and your wedding day style, but if the idea of making a wooden sign is too much, have no fear. There are plenty of online retailers like the artist and handmade community at Etsy.com, who will help you create one.

SEATING ARRANGEMENTS

There are really two ways to handle seating arrangements at your ceremony and reception: formal and informal. There is no right or wrong way, but it is best to make it clear to your guests as to where they should sit.

FORMAL

If you would like to assign guests to a table at the reception, then you should set up a place card or escort card table at the entrance where guests can find their seating location. When displaying the place cards, you have so many more options than the traditional white folded tented cards. One of the most popular ways to display these cards is on a clothesline with matching small clips or a by simply stringing them on some twine. Don't forget to add table numbers to your wedding tables that are easy to spot so that once your guests know where to sit they can find their way without too much hassle.

INFORMAL

If you are having an informal wedding, you might want to consider letting guests select their own table and seating at the reception. Since most guests will be looking for some direction as to where to sit, it is helpful to add a fun sign to inform guests of the casual arrangement.

TOP RIGHT: A bird motif is used in both the escort cards and the display around them.

BOTTOM RIGHT: A sign instructs guests to sit where they like as they enter the wedding celebration.

FACING, CLOCKWISE FROM TOP LEFT:
Birch logs are transformed into the perfect place card holder for a rustic chic wedding.

A slice of wood acts as a placeholder for escort cards and, when teamed up with simple objects like an apple, make for a wonderful country-style wedding look.

Birch tree slices are used to display the table numbers for each wedding table.

Hanging escort cards are displayed for guests using tiny clothespins and string.

Rustic escort cards adorned with twigs and a bird image are perfect for a barn wedding.

DECORATING BY SEASON

As the seasons change, so do the possibilities for wedding décor. By taking your cues from the season, your décor can include the natural elements in your surroundings to create a stunning barn wedding.

SPRING

The moment springtime comes, the intense wedding season starts to get underway. With all of nature starting to come out of the long winter slumber and bloom again, decorating for this season is almost effortless. All you really need to do is add large bursts of color.

Galvanized Buckets

Galvanized buckets and watering cans are a great way to give a nod to the gardening season and they allow for quick and easy flower displays. Easy to find and easy to display, these hardware store staples are a great choice for the spring season.

SUMMER

Since summer is the most popular season in which to get married, the inspiration and ideas are endless. Decorating for a summer wedding means taking into account the weather you might be encountering. If your barn does not have air-conditioning, then you should make sure you have other ways for guests to keep cool. Having large buckets of ice-cold water and paper fans or parasols are nice ways to make sure your guests are comfortable. Once you deal with these weather-related issues, you can move on to the countless beautiful décor ideas for the season.

FACING: *A birch wedding arbor is a great way to add a focal point to an outdoor wedding ceremony and allows the couple to exchange vows in rustic elegance.*

ABOVE: *Galvanized buckets with white and purple flowers are casually arranged for an outdoor wedding.*

ABOVE RIGHT: *Parasols, water and wedding programs are available for guests to take as they arrive to this outdoor farm wedding ceremony.*

FALL

Bring the outdoors in, by using a crisp autumn color palette and adding traditional fall items to your décor.

Pumpkins

Leave them in their natural orange color and stack them around the entrance to the barn, or scattered down long tables. If the color orange does not go with your theme, take on a DIY project and paint the exterior of the pumpkins white. Want to add some drama? Paint each pumpkin white, drill a few small holes in each one, and remove the tops. Pop a small candle in each and you get amazing wedding lanterns.

Apples

Much like the pumpkin, this traditional autumn symbol can look beautiful at weddings and might be an unexpected décor piece. First off, apples make a great and budget-friendly wedding favor. Simply place each shiny red apple in a clear bag, tie with some string and add a personalized tag. Beyond being just a great favor, apples make for one of the easiest decorating items since they look beautiful stacked up in baskets or crates.

WINTER

Many brides have the misconception that they have to select a summer or spring wedding date if they would like to have their wedding in a barn, but in reality there are plenty of barn venues that offer possibilities year round. The number one thing to consider when planning a barn wedding for the winter season is whether or not your facility will have the proper heating that you will need to keep your guests comfortable. With the staple colors of red and green, the winter season has infinite possibilities for décor that work beautifully in a barn setting.

Reds & Greens

Since the color of the season always comes back to some sort of red and green color theme, you have the chance to bring in some wonderful natural elements like berries, ferns, pine bows, and spruce sprigs.

FACING, TOP: Apples are a wonderful fall decoration to add to a wedding and can be used as centerpieces, favors or display items.

FACING, BOTTOM: An autumnal wedding display made of apples and apple crates looks perfectly rustic and elegant.

LEFT: A newly married wedding couple sits on the back of a pickup truck and shows off their new married status with a hanging wooden sign.

REAL
BARN WEDDINGS

- -

**THERE IS NOTHING QUITE LIKE ATTENDING
A WEDDING AND EXPERIENCING FIRSTHAND**
the unique way the couple has decided to celebrate. Each of
the real weddings featured in this section take an original and
personal approach to their ceremony and décor. However,
you'll find that these real weddings have a lot in common.
They are all set in picturesque locations where new discoveries
and creative ideas have been brought to life, showcasing the
best of barn wedding style. This is your exclusive invitation to
experience some of the most stunning barn weddings featuring
real couples, real emotion and real beauty.

WESTERN RANCH

THIS TEXAS RANCH WEDDING NOT ONLY OFFERS A
BEAUTIFUL BACKDROP BUT ALSO A UNIQUE BARN PERFECT
FOR A WESTERN RANCH-STYLE WEDDING, ALL THE WAY
DOWN TO A CAMPFIRE AND THE BRIDESMAID AND FLOWER
GIRL WRAPPED IN TRADITIONAL SADDLE BLANKET.
WITH A BEAUTIFUL OUTDOOR CEREMONY COMPLETE WITH
A BRIDE IN COWBOY BOOTS, FOLLOWED BY A BARN
RECEPTION WITH POPS OF TURQUOISE, THIS WEDDING
SHOWCASES WESTERN ELEGANCE AT ITS BEST.

ABOVE LEFT: *A flower girl in a simple white dress looks the country part in a denim jacket and cowboy boots.*

ABOVE: *Simple white baby's breath flowers are added to a classic milk jar and surrounded by antlers.*

FACING: *A happy bride and groom enter their rustic-style wedding reception.*

- -

PAGE 90: *Helping to add a natural perimeter to the wedding area are string lights and small cocktail tables, which focus the wedding activity towards the open-sided barn.*

PAGE 93: *A bonfire is a fun way to end a camp-style wedding and make this part of the evening also a tasty one by adding a s'more station close to the fire pit.*

Special wedding guests stand with the bride for a formal-style wedding picture.

ABOVE: *With a slab of rustic wood as the base, this simple yet elegant wedding centerpiece stands tall.*

ABOVE RIGHT: *A rustic sign points guests towards the wedding venue and celebration.*

ABOVE LEFT: *An array of flowers make up this wedding centerpiece and a touch of color is added with the blue vases.*

ABOVE: *A variety of pies are set out for guests to have a dessert. Along with traditional pies, this couple offered smaller pies in a jar.*

FACING: *Neutral table linens are paired with bright turquoise napkins, which add a pop of color to tables and match the vase in the centerpiece.*

FACING, LEFT: *A bride in a white sweater enjoys the reception part of her wedding with her new groom.*

FACING, RIGHT: *A small handmade sign marks the entrance to the cocktail time part of the evening at this wedding.*

ABOVE: *With string lights and a beautiful open building, this wedding has the best of both a barn wedding and an outdoor wedding.*

RIGHT: *Pinks, greens and a small touch of white make up the floral arrangements for this barn wedding centerpiece.*

FACING: *Bridesmaid and flower girl wrap themselves in a blanket to stay warm at this outdoor reception.*

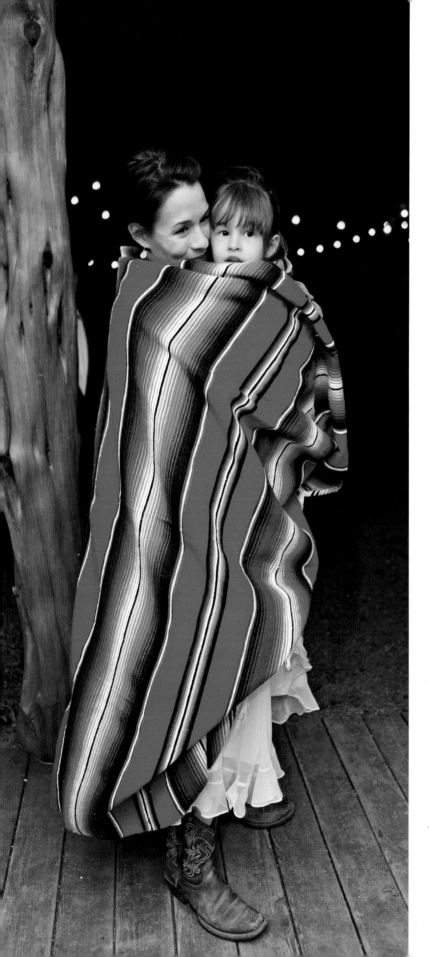

SOURCES

photography: Katherine O'Brien Photography / venue: Three Points Ranch,
Texas / event planner and designer: Christina Lewis, Wedding Warriors /
catering: BBQ Bill Archer & Silver K / pies: Tiny Pies / flowers: WOW Factor
Floral / rentals: DS Events, Dripping Springs, Bob's Outback Rentals

SPARKLING SPLENDOR

IF YOUR IDEA OF A BARN WEDDING IS ONE FILLED
WITH ELEGANCE AND SOPHISTICATION, THEN
THIS IS THE WEDDING FOR YOU. IN THIS AMAZING BARN
WEDDING, THE COUPLE CHOSE TO HOST BOTH THEIR
CEREMONY AND RECEPTION INSIDE THE BARN.
THANKS TO THE STUNNING ADDITION OF LARGE WHITE
DRAPES AND SPARKLING LIGHTS LINING TREE BRANCHES
AND BARN POSTS, THIS WEDDING SHOWS OFF A
TRULY ELEGANT AND DREAMY FEELING WHILE STAYING
TRUE TO THE RUSTIC SETTING.

ABOVE: *A white wedding bouquet filled with a mix of large and small blooms is ready for its debut.*

ABOVE RIGHT: *Bride and groom embrace in front of their barn wedding venue.*

- -

PAGE 105: *This couple enjoys their first dance.*

FACING, TOP: *Showcasing a couple's initials with large gold letters makes for a memorable vintage-style wedding picture.*

FACING, BOTTOM: *Wearing cowboy boots, the bride and groom take a moment for themselves.*

LEFT: *With a picturesque red barn and country-style white fence in the distance, this couple shares a kiss as husband and wife.*

ABOVE: *The complete bridal party flanks the bride and the groom in one large group shot.*

FACING, TOP: *This bridal party chose to wear cowboy boots with their purple bridesmaid dresses, and they look fantastic!*

FACING, BOTTOM: *A line of bridesmaids stands with small and delicate bouquets.*

RIGHT, TOP: *Tall branches with small white lights and striking drapery transform this barn into a fairytale-like wedding location.*

RIGHT, BOTTOM: *Using an old door as the display for the escort cards, this couple completes the countrified look by adding a burlap banner across the top.*

FACING, CLOCKWISE FROM TOP LEFT:
Adding a fun twist on the wedding desserts, this couple featured a trail mix bar at their wedding, allowing guests to fill up small bags and grab a snack for the road.

Guests dine at large round tables while the wedding party dines at one long table.

Collections of small floral arrangements are displayed on each table accompanied by the lace doily table number.

FACING: *A parade of guests lines the path to say farewell to the couple and light up the evening with sparklers.*

ABOVE: *The country bride and groom make their way from the wedding down the path to their new life together.*

SOURCES

photography: Miles Witt Boyer / venue: Pratt Place Inn & Barn / rentals: Festivities / catering: Krutons / florist: Rose of Sharron / dress designer: Allure Bridal / bridesmaid dresses: Amanda Archer / hair: Shang Salon / video: Imagine Film Company / cake designer: Shelby Lynn

COUNTRY QUILT

It's not every day that you come across a bride
who is so inspired by a classic country quilt
that it not only serves as the theme to her wedding
but is also incorporated into the gown. Weaving
together country charm with classic farm style,
this wedding features delicate décor items
such as vintage tablecloths, matched with original
style centerpieces like button-filled jars.

FACING, CLOCKWISE FROM TOP: *Happiness takes over this bride and groom as they share a celebratory moment.*

This wedding centerpiece showcases just how great a multi-piece arrangement can look.

A welcome chalkboard sign greets guests and informs them where the wedding will take place.

LEFT: *Hay is stacked up in a dark red barn that will act as the wedding venue.*

PAGE 117: *An item like a red pick-up truck can make for an impressive wedding picture prop.*

ABOVE: *A quilt pattern is featured on the back of this country-inspired wedding gown.*

ABOVE RIGHT: *A wildflower floral arrangement is complemented with a vintage-style tablecloth and small light blue pitcher.*

ABOVE: *Round tables with classic white chairs and floral design tablecloths create a country chic wedding atmosphere.*

ABOVE RIGHT: *A beautiful bride shows off the detailed work of her unique quilt-design wedding gown.*

FACING: *This bride and groom just tied the knot!*

ABOVE: *A quilt is hung from a clothesline and acts as a backdrop for the wedding.*

ABOVE RIGHT: *A classic country red pick-up truck is parked in a field adjacent to the wedding location.*

PAGE 123, TOP: *A country wedding couple shares a special moment in a picturesque setting.*

PAGE 123, BOTTOM: *A variety of glasses are set out for guests to take and toast to the bride and groom.*

SOURCES

photography: Kristyn Hogan / venue, styling and floral design: Historic Cedarwood / bride's
gown: Custom by Leeann Eubank / cake design: Patty Cakes / catering:
A Dream Come True Catering

GOLDEN MEADOWS

- -

Under the shade of a beautiful old tree surrounded
by the tranquil beauty of the countryside,
this simple yet chic wedding showcases how an
outside ceremony followed by a barn reception can
be the perfect combination. Using yellow as the
main color theme, carried out in the flowers, favors
and bridesmaid dresses, this country wedding shines
like the sun. With sweet sentiments like asking
guests to "choose a seat and not a side" proudly
displayed on a chalkboard as guests enter the
ceremony, this wedding couldn't be more endearing.

PAGE 127: *A bride stands ready for her day with her bridesmaids and young flower girls.*

FACING, TOP: *Yellow bridesmaid dresses mimic the beautiful color of the wheat field.*

FACING, BOTTOM: *The bride carries the yellow theme of her wedding by adding yellow shoes to her wedding day style.*

ABOVE: *There is nothing more romantic than a wedding under the shade of a large tree.*

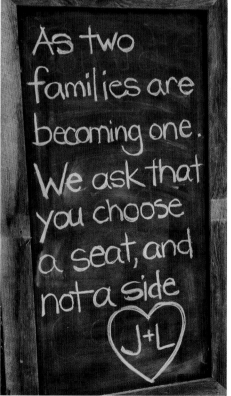

As two families are becoming one. We ask that you choose a seat, and not a side J+L

ABOVE: *Bridesmaids in sunny yellow dresses surround a bride on her wedding day.*

FACING: *A sunflower bouquet is wrapped in burlap fabric and really stands out against the bride's white gown.*

-- --

PAGE 130, CLOCKWISE FROM TOP: *A country display complete with burlap and rustic signs acts as the perfect gift table.*

A simple note on a framed chalkboard informs guests to sit where they like at the ceremony.

The favors for this table are stacked, waiting for guests to take them on their way out of the reception.

PAGE 131, TOP: *Surrounded by candlelight, a rustic wedding cake is displayed.*

PAGE 131, BOTTOM: *Soft lighting is used to make this barn space feel intimate and sophisticated.*

FACING: Holding a lantern, this bride and groom embrace in a tender moment.

ABOVE: A hanging chandelier is a wonderful juxtaposition in this rustic barn space.

ABOVE RIGHT: A southern country bride and groom meet under a tree.

SOURCES

photography: Dove Wedding Photography / venue: Vinewood, Georgia / catering:
Kimbles Food by Design / floral design: Sweet Pea's of LaGrange / cake design: Cakes
by Debbie

SOUTHERN COMFORT

A SUN-FILLED WEDDING DAY SETS THE STAGE FOR
A GORGEOUS OUTDOOR WEDDING CEREMONY FOLLOWED BY
A BARN WEDDING COMPLETE WITH STRING LIGHTS,
MISMATCHED CHAIRS, AND WHITE FARMHOUSE-STYLE
PITCHERS FOR FLOWERS. THIS WEDDING HAS PERFECT
SOUTHERN SOPHISTICATION WITH THE BRIDESMAIDS
ALL CARRYING PARASOLS AND THE COUPLE
SHARING AN END-OF-THE-EVENING KISS UNDER A TREE
FILLED WITH FLICKERING MASON JARS.

RICIA STANKO & DANIEL BROWN

9.24.11

WEDDING PARTY

MAID OF HONOR
Rachel Troy

BRIDESMAIDS
Nicole Good
Lauren Ledford
Lexsie Oliver

FLOWER GIRL
Maddie Brown

BEST MAN
Stephen Brown

GROOMSMEN
P.J. Stanko
Dan Yetter
Reid Dannville

RING BEARER
Elijah Brown

PARENTS
LINDA & PAUL STANKO

VICKIE & DAVI... BROWN

THE CEREMONY

Prelude: Whatever it is - Zac Brown
Processional: Rhythm of Love - Plain White Tees
Processional of the Bride: Here Comes the Sun - The Beatl...
Welcome: Rev. Kenny Schmitt
Prayer
Presentation
Reading: Ethel Oliver
Charge
Vows
Rings
Pronouncement
Presentation of the Bride and Groom
Recessional: I'm Yours - Jason Mraz

I love you not only for what you are, but for what I am when I am with you. I love you not only for what you have ... yourself, but for what yo... ...k... ...g of me ... part... ...k ...brin...

FACING: *A bridesmaid in a coral-colored dress holds her blooming bouquet.*

ABOVE: *Under a shower of rose petals, the bride and groom make their way from the reception.*

- -

PAGE 137: *The wedding ceremony program and bridal party listing is printed on beautiful kraft paper.*

FACING, TOP: *Bridesmaids stand with parasols in this sun-filled outdoor wedding ceremony.*

FACING, BOTTOM: *A joyful bride and groom make their way down the outdoor aisle, which is surrounded by mismatched chairs.*

LEFT, TOP: *A mix of long and round tables await the guests at this wedding reception held in a barn.*

LEFT, BOTTOM: *White pitchers, a country staple, are the perfect barn wedding centerpiece.*

FACING, CLOCKWISE FROM TOP LEFT: *A green plant stand showcases wedding cupcakes and also displays the message of the day: love.*

One large floral arrangement in a rustic display marks the entrance to a wedding reception.

White pitchers tied with twine are the perfect centerpiece for these burlap-covered tables.

ABOVE: *Adding a vintage touch to a barn wedding can be as easy as mixing and matching chair styles at the wedding tables.*

FACING: *A bride in a strapless, A-line style gown stands with her husband as the sun shines.*

ABOVE: *Leaving their wedding in a vintage convertible, the bride and groom drive towards their future together.*

SOURCES

photography: Sean and Amanda Photography/ venue: Vinewood, Georgia / floral design: Blueberry / cake designer: Sweet Sensations / bridesmaid dress: Bari Jay/ logo designer: Set Apart Designs

TIPS FROM THE PROS

- -

SINCE BECOMING A BLOGGER IN 2009, I've had many opportunities to feature amazing weddings and wedding ideas, and I love being able to introduce my readers to wedding experts who can help add a sense of direction. In this section I call on some of my favorite and most trusted wedding experts to help you plan your barn wedding. Find out what Chelsea and Virginia, event planners with Bluebird Productions, have to say about planning a barn wedding. Then get beauty advice from celebrity beauty expert and founder of Farm Couture, Cat Ianelli. Lisa and Stephanie Karvellas from Cedar Lakes Estates also offer advice on barn wedding venues, and, finally, get expert dress advice from Chelsea Tyler-McNamara, owner of Everthine Bridal Boutique.

TIPS FROM EVENT PLANNERS

CHELSEA & VIRGINIA OF BLUEBIRD PRODUCTIONS

Chelsea VanVleet Dillon and Virginia Frischkorn created Bluebird Productions because they saw a need for an environmentally friendly event concierge company in Aspen, Snowmass and the Roaring Fork Valley in Colorado. After working for many Aspen wedding planners at various Aspen wedding venues, Chelsea and Virginia noticed excess waste created as a byproduct of the event industry. Find more information about Bluebird Productions at Bluebirdaspen.com.

TOP 10 THINGS TO REMEMBER WHEN PLANNING A BARN WEDDING

1. Barns are not always a standard shape, so make sure you think about the layout and your floor plan before you invite more people than you can accommodate.

2. Think about the senses. Barns can be stinky, so make sure it is aired out before you start setting up for the wedding. Burlap can be stinky as well but can make very fun tablecloths or table runners. Lay burlap flat and air it out for a few days beforehand.

3. Use unique items you can find in or around the barn such as old wagons for beverage/food stations, old farming tools to decorate the escort card table or find items that are rustic and fit the theme such as mason jars and twine.

4. Keep it local. Barns are the perfect venue for a green or farm-to-table wedding. Think about using local produce, meat, and flowers for your barn wedding.

5. No smoking! Barns are normally made of wood and have hay around. Barns can go up in flames very quickly. If it is necessary to have a designated smoking area, make sure this area is away from the barn. Provide proper fire extinguishers.

6. Lighting. Barns oftentimes have minimal lighting, so this is something to think about. Twinkle lights can look beautiful strung from rafters or you can get creative and hang mason jars with LED lights in them.

7. Bathrooms. Does the barn have bathrooms? If so, can it accommodate the number of guests attending your wedding? If you need to rent porta-potties, research what kind and how many stalls you need and get a few quotes.

8. Think about ventilation. It can get very hot inside the barn, especially if you add candles and 150 people with body heat.

9. Music. Country or bluegrass bands can be fun for barn weddings. Think about where you will have room for your band and if you need an A/V company to bring power in for the band.

10. Bugs. Horses and fields can be very buggy. Be prepared with bug spray for the guests and citronella candles.

THE IDEAL TIMELINE FOR PLANNING A BARN WEDDING

Here at Bluebird Productions, an Aspen-based event-planning firm, we love weddings that involve a barn. A barn is the perfect backdrop or venue for a rustic chic wedding. Barns set a beautiful tone for an exquisite wedding.

We believe in planning ahead as much as possible. That way, should something unexpected happen in your life, you are prepared and your wedding doesn't get pushed to the wayside. Also, there is nothing worse than realizing you are two months out and not being able to book your dream band! Follow this timeline for your ideal barn wedding:

12 Months Out

☐ Determine your guest list and budget. Remember to keep these things paramount while starting your search. Get ready to dig in!

☐ Find your perfect barn! Is your barn going to hold the reception or be the perfect backdrop for your ceremony or reception?

☐ Start interviewing caterers.

11 Months Out

☐ Secure your caterer.

☐ Secure your photographer.

☐ Get bids from tent and party rental companies. What does your caterer include? What does the barn already have?

☐ Who doesn't love flowers? Get your date on hold with a florist and start coming up with your vision. Remember that it may change but make sure you have a florist secured.

10 Months Out

☐ Secure an officiant (someone to marry you!)— Think about the flow of the ceremony and whether you will want any readers in the ceremony.

☐ Start looking into bands and/or DJs for the reception. Don't wait too long!

☐ Think about ceremony music—have you always dreamed of a string trio or quartet, or does an acoustic guitar sound more up your alley?

9 Months Out

☐ Does your barn have restrooms that you can use? If not, it's time to think about porta-potties.

☐ Book your band!

☐ Does your band have extra energy and lighting requirements or do they bring their own? Some barns look amazing with twinkle lights strung across the ceiling, some barns really pop when you do extra lighting, and some look amazing with an entire light show. It might be time to look at an audio-visual/ lighting company.

8 Months Out

☐ Send out save the dates. Incorporate your barn onto the save the date! Perhaps the barn doors are part of the card and they open up to have the information.

☐ Does your barn have enough electricity to handle the band you just booked? Talk to the A/V company you booked about adding a generator if needed.

7 Months Out

☐ Interested in a videographer? Research the options and book a videographer if you would like to document your wedding in this manner.

☐ What do you want to drink on your big day? Will you have an open bar or just beer, wine, champagne and a specialty cocktail? Look into options for sourcing the alcohol. Don't order until you have a clearer sense on your head count but be ready to go once you do. There is plenty to do in the final months, so the more you can be prepared the better.

6 Months Out

☐ Secure a pastry chef to bake your wedding cake or create your dessert display. Remember that the sky is the limit with wedding desserts these days. Don't feel that you need to be locked into a white buttercream cake.

☐ Revisit your floral vision.

☐ Time to book hair and makeup for the big day! Remember to schedule a practice. Schedule the practice as to the wedding as possible so that you (and the stylist) remember exactly what you like.

5 Months Out

☐ Work on your menu with a caterer. Think about what will be in season at the time of your wedding. Remember to consider the presentation of the meal.

☐ Do you need transportation to and from your venue for your guests? Look into mass transportation options if needed.

☐ How will all the garbage be removed from your barn? Does the caterer remove it? This isn't a very glamorous part of a wedding, but it certainly is an important detail.

4 Months Out

☐ Work on a song list for the band. You'll want to give them ample time to perfect your first dance, father/daughter dance, and mother/son dance, so don't wait until the last minute!

☐ Work on your songs for the ceremony.

3 Months Out

☐ It's time to think about some of the fun details: guest book, napkin folds, place settings, table numbers and favors.

☐ Finalize rental orders.

2 Months Out

☐ Send out your invitations (six to eight weeks is standard). RSVPs should be due three to four weeks before the big day.

☐ Work on your "must get" photo lists with your photographer.

1 Month to Go!

☐ Finalize your "paper goods": escort cards, programs, menus, etc. There are so many fun and rustic options that aren't always "paper." Think outside the box and look to things like chalkboards, slate, vintage glass windows and mason jars with painted numbers.

TIPS FROM THE BEAUTY EXPERT

CATHERINE IANELLI OF FARM COUTURE

Catherine Ianelli is an esthetician and founder of Farm Couture, a boutique skin care company. Well known for her vibrant talent, expertise and ten years within the beauty industry, she also was the beauty contributor featured in the book *Rustic Wedding Chic*. Find more information about Farm Couture at Farmcoutre.com.

BARN BRIDE BEAUTY

Whitewashed wooden frames, sun-bleached floors, crooked barn doors, scattered wild flowers, lofty ceilings aimed towards the sky, soft textures and grasses swaying against the breeze are all defining details of a barn wedding. As a bride you want to be the glowing center of attention, yet delicately blend with the vintage foundation, whimsy and romance that only a barn can so beautifully offer.

Even with the natural charm and textural allure of a barn wedding, you are the signature centerpiece as the bride. With such an incredible backdrop and editorial location, you want your beauty to radiate. Barn weddings clearly create a unique story and with a few simple expert beauty tips, you will be radiating barn bride beauty!

Follow a Good Skin Care Routine

- ☐ In the mornings and at night, use a gentle cleanser that will properly cleanse your skin without drying it out.

- ☐ At night, use a nourishing eye make-up remover along with cleanser.

- ☐ Use a moisturizer daily morning and night—your skin needs nourishment just like your body does! A hydrating serum will add moisture and give you that bridal glow.

- ☐ Use a quality, gentle exfoliant to help shed dull, dead skin at least twice a week to keep the skin fresh and smooth.

BROW BEAUTIFUL

Get your brows groomed by a professional. It will make you look instantly polished with a professional eyebrow shaping. Have your brows done a few days before the wedding so they don't look red or bumpy on the big day. It will make such a difference in photos to have perfect brows!

BRIDE BEAUTY MAKEUP

FACE

I would recommend that you focus on a natural, clean, soft, delicate look. In selecting a foundation/base, avoid shimmer. Less shimmer means better photography. Shimmer may look fabulous in person, but it can often reflect too much in photos, causing you to have white spots or look washed out/too bright. It may accentuate wrinkles or problem areas, too. Opt for "adult shimmer" if you must, which is mostly ultra-fine shimmer that goes on evenly and subtly.

WATERPROOF

Choose matte and waterproof cosmetics for your wedding day look. Light-reflective makeup, particularly shimmery glosses or blushes, may make your skin appear shiny in photographs. Also, waterproof cosmetics will stay put through heat, rain or tears.

FOCAL FEATURE

Highlight one facial feature. Choose your favorite feature and make it the star of your wedding day makeup look. A beautiful eye, bold lip or enhanced cheekbones will look stunning against a neutral backdrop, but will compete with one another if all are employed.

Beauty Tip: For super-soft lips, mix a little sugar with honey and make a paste. Apply mixture gently to lips and massage in circular motion. Rinse and wipe with a warm washcloth and pat dry. Lips will be prepped for lipstick, gloss and of course for your groom!

HERE COMES THE SUN

HEAT FACTOR

Stash baby wipes in the bathroom to freshen up. Dancing it up barn style is clearly a great time, but it's not so elegant when someone goes to give you a hug and you are over heated. I recommend using baby wipes to freshen up. They're also great for getting out stains in a pinch without leaving a big ring like water can.

SPF

Important as SPF is, note that SPF often reflects light in photographs, which will make your face appear lighter than the rest of you (or wash you out). I always advise you to skip the SPF for this one occasion if it's possible. If you burn easily and have an outdoor wedding, I suggest using Laura Mercier primer, because it is a primer so it'll be layered with foundation and powder without SPF so it shouldn't reflect light, especially since outdoor weddings do not utilize flash as often (and having to wear SPF is usually a concern for those having an outdoor wedding).

UMBRELLA SHADE

If you're going to be taking outdoor pictures during the hours of 12:00 p.m. to 2:00 p.m., carry an umbrella to shield your face from the sun. In addition, pack an emergency kit, which you can give to your mom or maid of honor for safekeeping. It should include a compact, a lipstick, powder-free blotting papers to remove shine, and a small tube of concealer with a tiny synthetic brush for quick touchups.

NATURALLY PRETTY NAILS

Avoid bold nail polish. Your hands will be on stage for the entire day signing the certificate, showing off your rings, shaking hands, and you'll want them looking feminine. You want to avoid painting your nails a color like BURGUNDY, because you won't want to cringe every time you look at your wedding pictures Do yourself a favor and choose a pretty pale pink or nude for your wedding day manicure.

MORNING OF THE WEDDING

A very common secret behind the glowing skin is excessive use of water, especially early morning before taking breakfast.

Apply a Gel Mask

Gel masks are water based so they won't add any oil to the skin (which can interfere with wedding day makeup). They calm the skin, soothe away redness caused from wedding day nerves and smooth the skin. Leave on the mask for ten minutes, rinse and apply an oil-free mattifying lotion. Proceed with makeup.

Drink a Lot of Water

To prevent skin from puffiness due to shedding tears or alcohol intake the night before, drink ice water throughout the day. This will also help prevent your mouth from getting dry due to nerves.

Practice Deep Breathing

There is nothing better to calm the nerves than frequent deep breaths. Relax and enjoy yourself. Your day is here.

TIPS FROM BARN WEDDING VENUE OWNERS

lisa & stephanie karvellas
of cedar lakes estate

Stephanie and Lisa's earliest memories were on the grounds of Cedar Lakes Estate. Growing up here was any child's dream— white Christmases, fresh mountain air and lazy lakeside summer days make up the fabric of their childhood. The sisters returned to Cedar Lakes and decided to build a business where they could foster their love for food, event planning, and affection for their childhood home. Now as the estate's co-founders, they work each day to share their combined passions with their visitors. Find more information about Cedar Lakes Estate at cedarlakesestate.com.

Casual elegance. Luxury nestled in the rolling countryside. There is simply no other wedding venue as timeless and expressive as a beautiful barn. The wide-open space, simplicity, and charm provide the perfect backdrop for a magical and completely customizable wedding. What better place to celebrate marriage than in a setting that evokes a sense of tradition, stability and excitement?

To ensure your wedding day is as timeless as the venue itself, here are seven tips for creating a uniquely enchanting event:

1 **Make the space your own.**

Since a barn is typically an immense building with high ceilings and minimal accents, this is your chance to showcase your personality. In such a vast space, the sky's the limit—go for it! Whether it's genteel greenery or decadent floral arrangements, always make sure the room transforms into a reflection of you.

2. **Remember lighting.**

Most barns have very minimal lighting, so plan ahead to find the perfect balance of practicality and aesthetics. Purchase a few different bulb options to see which hue and wattage works best with the barn's interior. Test the lights well in advance for location and brightness and ensure the bulbs will last through the night. Don't forget to vary the type of lighting you use. A mix of focused, ambient and reflected light works best.

3 **Think outside the box.**

You're having a wedding at a completely unique venue, but don't stop your creativity there. Use reclaimed objects to contrast the elegance of the day. Who says an old chicken wire fence isn't beautiful for hanging place cards and a hay bale draped with lace isn't a suitable ceremony seat?

4 **Focus on small nuances and personal touches.**

A truly magnificent wedding is one that focuses on the small, personal touches. Whether it's a rosemary sprig in the napkins, butcher's twine around cupcake boxes, or burlap bows around the chairs, these details are what paint a beautiful and unforgettable memory.

5. **Make a large space feel intimate.**

A barn's cathedral-like ceiling is what makes it magnificent and dramatic, but this sometimes could also make the space feel impersonal. Hang string lights or drapery above the tables at around twelve feet. This creates the illusion of a lower ceiling height and adds cozy warmth to the space without compromising the breathtaking expanse of the building.

6. **Add color and texture.**

The beautiful bone structure of a barn is the perfect canvas for the color palette that reflects your personality and style. Muted earth tones or mixing splashy patterns, organic materials or geometric shapes can set the stage for the bride to shine. Try to group small selections of color and texture together and repeat them throughout the room.

7. **Highlight the rustic-chic juxtaposition.**

Maintaining the balance between the rustic and elegant elements of your wedding is absolutely critical. There's a certain feeling evoked when seeing chipped, reclaimed barn wood next to gorgeous white lace. It is this impression that helps create the perfect atmosphere for a memorable barn wedding. If you focus too much on one end of the spectrum, the feeling is lost. The elegant décor you bring to the barn should never attempt to cover up the rustic charm but instead enhance it.

TIPS FROM A WEDDING DRESS EXPERT

CHELSEA TYLER-MCNAMARA OF EVERTHINE BRIDAL BOUTIQUE

A graduate from Parsons School of Design, Chelsea went on to pursue fashion public relations and styling in New York City. Her passion for fashion broadened when the love of her life, Tim, popped the question. Chelsea soon became head over heels in love with all things non-traditional bridal. Disappointed in what area bridal shops had to offer, Chelsea set out to provide brides like herself an intimate bridal-shopping experience with a unique gown selection that can't be found anywhere else. She opened Everthine Bridal Boutique in 2011, featuring hard-to-find designers like Jenny Packham, Claire Pettibone, Sarah Seven, and more all under one roof. Find more information about Everthine Bridal Boutique at Shopeverthine.com.

10 TIPS FOR SHOPPING FOR YOUR BARN WEDDING GOWN

1. Have an open mind! Nine times out of ten, the bride chooses a dress that she never thought she'd like. Sometimes what you want might not look good on your particular shape, so trust your stylist's eye and be open to trying on different shapes and styles.

2. No buts! We always tell our brides that there should be "no buts" about her dress. If you like the dress, BUT aren't sure about the beading, then it's not your dress! This is YOUR day. You should feel 100 percent confident in your dress decision.

3. Paint the picture. Visualize your setting, the surroundings, and your future husband waiting for you at the end of the aisle. Is your dress blowing in the summer wind? Are the night stars reflecting off the beading on your dress? Think about your setting and how your dress fits into your picture-perfect day. This will help narrow your decision and ultimately find "the one!"

4. Complement your setting. Barns have intricate and imperfect qualities that rustic brides adore. Choose a dress with the same elements! Many of our dresses have intricate details such as raw edges and asymmetrical hemlines, allowing them to tie in with a barn's lovely surroundings.

5. Do your research. Before you shop, make sure your boutique carries designers and styles you like and find yourself drawn to. At Everthine, we cater to a more laid-back bride looking for a dress with vintage touches and a bohemian spirit. No cake-toppers here! Finding your dress should be fun and exciting. Don't set yourself up for disappointment by making an appointment at a shop that isn't your taste.

6. Choose your entourage wisely. We suggest leaving the entourage behind and bringing with you one or two guests who know YOU and YOUR style best. Chat with them before your appointment and let them in on your vision and what you're looking for. Make them aware of the barn venue and the rustic qualities you love. Don't be afraid of letting them know that this is ultimately your decision and they are there for support. Advice should only be given when asked.

7. Accessorize your hair! Brides often forget that a headpiece can really put the finishing touch to their wedding day look. We absolutely adore floral halos for barn weddings. Whether your florist designs one out of real flowers or you purchase a ready-made one, they are the perfect way to add a delicate bohemian touch to an outdoor celebration.

8. Shop smart! Jenny Packham, Sarah Seven, Claire Pettibone and Elizabeth Dye are just a few designers whose gowns lend themselves beautifully to barn weddings. If you find yourself loving one designer in particular, make sure to find out when a boutique in your area will be hosting a trunk show. Boutiques only carry a curated selection of each designer's collections. During a trunk show, the entire collection will be available to try on and discounts are often given!

9. To train or not to train. Many barn weddings take place outdoors. When choosing a dress with a train, it's important to think about whether or not it will drag in the grass or a dirt area. Are you able to bustle the dress to avoid this? Will you be able to dance with it behind you? Either way, make sure to think about whether or not a train is something you'd love or want to avoid.

10. Give yourself enough time! Gowns typically can take anywhere from six to nine months to arrive. Yes, this seems like way in advance, but trust me when I tell you it's a huge sign of relief! Once you find your dress, choosing other elements such as flowers and linens make the planning process even more fun!

PHOTO CREDITS & RESOURCES

All websites listed are accurate at the time of publication but are subject to change.

- -

PHOTOGRAPHERS

Afterglow Photos
   afterglowphotos.com

Brooke Boling: Back cover top right and top left, 2, 65–77, 82 right
   brookeboling.com

Dove Wedding Photography: 18 middle, 19 left, 83 bottom right, 127–135, 146, 149 left
   doveweddingphotography.com

Harper Point Photography: 6 top, 12 right, 13 middle, 14, 80 bottom left, 84 bottom
   harperpoint.com

John Schnack Photography: 10 top, 13 bottom right, 17
   johnschnack.com

Joyeuse Photography: 41–47, 87 left
   joyeusephotography.com

Kate Holstein Photography: 148
   kateholstein.com

Katherine O'Brien: 90, 93–103
   katherineobrien.com

Katelyn James Photography: Cover
   katelynjames.com

Kristyn Hogan: 10 bottom, 18 bottom, 25–39, 78, 80 bottom right, 117–125
   kristynhogan.com

Laura Leigh Photo: 83 top right, 89
   lauraleighphoto.com

Maggie Carson Romano: Author's photo
   mcr-photography.com

Melissa McCrotty Photography: 6 bottom, 22, 49–63, 152
   melissamccrotty.com

Michelle Gardella Photography: 156
   michellegardella.com

Miles Witt Boyer: 21 left, 105–115
   mileswittboyer.com

Orchard Cove Photography: Back cover bottom left and bottom right; 9 top left, top right, bottom; 12 left; 13 top; 13 bottom left; 16; 21 right; 80 top right; 81 right; 82 left; 83 left; 84 top; 85–86; 87 right; 88; 149 right; 153
   orchardcovephotography.com

Sean and Amanda: 18 top, 19 right, 80 top left, 81 left, 137–145
   seanandamanda.com

Tom Moore Photo: 151
   tommoorephoto.com

VENUES

Cedar Lakes Estate: cedarlakesestate.com

Historic Cedarwood: cedarwoodweddings.com

Old Hickory Lake: cedarcreekyachtclub.com

Pratt Place Inn & Barn: prattplaceinn.com

Rounton Farm: rountonfarm.com

Southall Eden: southalleden.com

The Barn At Twin Oaks: barnattwinoaksranch.wix.com/home

Three Points Ranch: threepointsranch.com

Vinewood: vinewoodevents.com

Virginia Barn Wedding/Adams International School: facebook.
com/VirginiaBarnWeddingAdamsInternationalSchool

WEDDING & EVENT DETAILS

Hey Babe Studio: heybabestudio.com

Jenni Bowlin: jennibowlin.com

Shabby Love: shabbylovefurniture.com

ANTIQUES & VINTAGE RESOURCES

Bushwick Hardware: etsy.com/shop/BushwickHardware

LionShare Antique: lionshareantiques.com

Salvage Wrights: salvagewrights.com

EVENT DESIGN & COORDINATION

Amber Housley: amberhousley.com

Amore Events by Cody: amoreeventsbycody.com

Bluebird Productions: bluebirdaspen.com

Historic Cedarwood: cedarwoodweddings.com

Rambling House Events: ramblinghouseevents.com

Southall Eden: southalleden.com

Wedding Warriors: theweddingwarriors.com

FLORAL DESIGN

Blueberry Spring: blueberryspring.com

Brocade Designs: brocadenashville.com

Colonial Florist: colonialfloristandantiques.com

Rose of Sharon: roseofsharon-eventflorist.com

Sweet Pea's of LaGrange: sweetpeasoflagrange.com

The Enchanted Florist: enchantedfloristtn.com

CATERING

A Dream Come True Catering: adctcatering.com

Beggars Banquet: beggarsbanquetcatering.com

Kimble's Food by Design: kimblesfood.com

Krutons: krutonscatering.com

Silver K Café: silverkcafe.com

BEAUTY

Amy Lynn Larwig: amylynnlarwig.com

Farm Couture: farmcouture.com

Neil Robison: johndavidagency.com/neilrobison

CAKE DESIGN & SWEETS

Cakes by Debbie: cakesbydebbie.net

Crumb de la crumb: crumbdelacrumb.com

Greenock Bakery: greenockbakery.com

Patty Cakes: pattycakes-tn.com

Shelby Lynn: shelbylynnscakeshoppe.com

Sweet Sensations: sweet-sensations.com

Tiny Pies: tinypies.com

The Cake Place: thecakeplacebakery.com

FASHION

Allure Bridals: allurebridals.com

Amanda Archer: etsy.com/shop/amandaarcher

Bari Jay: barijay.com

Billy Reid: billyreid.com

Everthine Bridal Boutique: shopeverthine.com

Formal Affairs: allformalaffairs.com

Low's Bridal: lowsbridal.com

Monique Lhuillier: moniquelhuillier.com

Reeme Acra: reemacra.com

Watters: watters.com

RENTAL COMPANIES

Festivities Tents and Events: festivitiestentsandevents.com

Gibson Rental: gibsonrental.com

VIDEO SERVICES

Imagine Film Company: imaginefilmcompany.com

STATIONERY

Set Apart Designs: etsy.com/shop/SetApartDesigns85

ONLINE RESOURCES

Etsy: etsy.com

Rustic Wedding Guide: rusticweddingguide.com

Whispering Pines Catalog: whisperingpinescatalog.com